new
metal foil crafts

SIMPLE AND INSPIRING CRAFTS TO MAKE AT HOME

GLOUCESTER MASSACHUSETTS

ROCKPORT PUBLISHERS

BARBARA **MATTHIESSEN**

© 2002 by Rockport Publishers, Inc.

First published in the United States of America by
Rockport Publishers, Inc.
33 Commercial Street
Gloucester, Massachusetts 01930-5089
Telephone: (978) 282-9590
Fax: (978) 283-2742
www.rockpub.com

Library of Congress Cataloging-in-Publication Data

Matthiessen, Barbara.
    New metal foil crafts : simple and inspiring crafts to make at home/
Barbara Matthiessen.
        p. cm.
    ISBN 1-56496-898-7
    1. aluminum foil craft. I. Title.
TT242 .M28 202
745.5—dc21   2002004583

10 9 8 7 6 5 4 3 2 1

Design: Rule 29
Cover Image: Bobbie Bush Photography, www.bobbiebush.com

Printed in Singapore

10/02
BH

contents

introduction

Working with metal has traditionally been the domain of blacksmiths, tinsmiths, goldsmiths, and silversmiths. Metalworking tools, from high-temperature furnaces to welding torches, can be intimidating. However, thanks to a new product—metal foil—crafting with metal is no longer beyond the means of the average crafter and artisan. Anyone—even children—can now make original metal projects.

In the first chapter, you'll learn about the different types of metal foil and wire available to crafters. You'll also learn about ways to construct and embellish metal foil. Be sure to read the section on various joining processes, such as folding, wiring, and gluing foils together and to other materials. In the section covering embellishments, you'll read about surface treatments, such as paints, stamps, and patinas.

Eighteen step-by-step projects will guide you through the process of creating useful items for every room in your home, as well as gifts you can be proud to give, such as lamp shades, frames, journals, vases, wreaths, lanterns, and sculptures. As you make these attractive and functional projects, you'll learn and practice techniques that you can apply to other materials and future projects.

A gallery containing intriguing projects from a number of talented designers has been provided to further inspire you. These projects illustrate the great range of effects you can achieve with metal foils. Allow the gallery projects to encourage you to explore and express your own creativity with this new and exciting medium.

CHAPTER ONE

basics

METAL FOIL & WIRE

types of foil

Foils are classified by three criteria: their gauge, or thickness; surface treatment; and base metal. Reactions to surface treatments, strength, and workability vary with foil types. For these reasons, you need to understand the characteristics of the foil you select for your project.

foil gauges

The thickness of metal foil is expressed either by gauge or by the thousandths of an inch or millimeter. Gauge is measured by number, and the higher the gauge, the thinner the foil. Most foils are classified as 30-gauge or higher. Foils listed in millimeters vary in thickness from 0.0012 mm thick to 0.005 mm. The lower-gauge, or thicker, foils are commonly sold as "tooling foils." For more intricate designs (with finer detail), use a higher-gauge, or thinner, foil.

foil surface treatments

Manufacturers supply a variety of surface treatments on foil, ranging from nothing to various colored inks and durable plastic lamination. Without a surface treatment, some foils oxidize over time, developing their own patina. A clear-coated finish allows the natural color of the foil to remain unchanged over time. Colored foil is coated with inks, which give the foil its color. Laminated foil is available in different colors and prints, as well as in natural metal tones, with the lamination also serving to strengthen the foil.

metal bases for foils

ALUMINUM FOIL is available in a wide range of gauges, and is easy to cut and manipulate into different shapes. Repeated bending weakens it, causing it to become brittle, and can lead to cracking. Aluminum resists oxidation, so traditional patina techniques do not work on it.

COPPER FOIL is also easy to work with, but it also becomes brittle and will crack with repeated bending. If left untreated, copper develops a natural patina.

BRASS FOIL is more difficult to cut and manipulate than aluminum and copper foil. Brass foil, which is made of an alloy of copper and tin, easily becomes brittle, and it resists many surface treatments. Brass foil is much stiffer and more difficult to emboss than a similarly gauged aluminum or copper foil

PEWTER FOIL is not made of true pewter but a tin alloy. Pewter foil is pliable and can be cut and embossed easily. It develops a soft, natural patina over time.

STEEL TOOLING FOIL is a heavier foil often sold as "Rusty Tin." Steel foil is durable, making it ideal for items that will be used frequently. You can punch steel foil, but embossing is next to impossible. Cut this foil into shapes and allow it to rust naturally, or speed up the rusting process with apple cider vinegar.

types of wire

Wire is an important material in metal foil crafting and is often used as a construction device and as an embellishment. Many types of wire are available, ranging in color, composition, and size. Wire size is expressed in gauge numbers, with the smallest gauge number being the largest in diameter. The most common range for wire is 14-gauge to 36-gauge. Copper, steel, aluminum, brass, and alloy wires are available, untreated or with special coatings. Copper-core wire, which is available in 25 colors and in three gauges, has vinyl coating, is kind to the hands, and is easy to work. Art supply stores, craft stores, and hardware stores are all good sources for wires.

TOOLS & TECHNIQUES

working with metal

Crafting with metal foil and wire is safe when you practice common sense. Always wear gloves and safety glasses when working with heavier foil and wire or when using power tools. Work on a well-lit surface that can be easily cleared of small foil and wire pieces. Use all tools properly, and refer to the manufacturer's instructions where needed.

Metal under stress, such as a twisted wire, develops a tension that when released can cause the metal to spring in unexpected ways. When working with a stressed metal, be sure to wear safety glasses and contain the metal or cover it with something, such as a gloved hand, before releasing the tension.

Some metals have toxic reactions to certain chemicals. Use only supplies intended for metal or those certified by the Arts and Crafts Institute as "nontoxic." Be sure to read and follow the manufacturer's instructions carefully.

using tools for working with foil

Many of the tools you'll need to work with metal foil are common household items: a straightedge ruler, scissors, permanent markers, dry ballpoint pen, and masking tape. You will also need old magazines or a phone book to provide a padded work surface. A number of the projects in this book can be completed with these tools alone.

MEASURING, MARKING, AND SCORING

When working with metal foil, apply the adage "measure twice and cut once." A metal ruler is the most accurate measuring and scoring tool, but you can also use measuring tapes, standard rulers, and yardsticks. T squares and carpenters' squares are also helpful, because they can be used for measuring and for keeping corners square and lines parallel.

Test markers or grease pencils on a scrap of foil first to see if the marks will remain for the length of time that you need them. If you want the marks to be visible in the finished project, use permanent markers or dye-based inks.

The preferred method for marking metal foils is to lightly score or scribe design lines directly onto the foil. Hold your straightedge firmly on the foil or tape your pattern onto the foil, and then run your embossing tool along the straightedge or around the pattern lines. These lines should be considered permanent—removing them is impossible on some foils. You can also lay carbon paper between your pattern and the metal foil, and trace over the design lines with an embossing tool.

To score the foil to make a fold line, you must scratch the surface of the foil but not go through it. A stylus, awl, fine embossing tool, or dry ballpoint pen all make excellent scoring tools. Hold or tape your straightedge or template firmly to the foil, and then run your scoring tool along the edges.

CUTTING

A pair of household scissors is all you need for cutting most metal foil. Thicker foil may require utility or metal shears or tin snips. Make sure your scissors are sharp, and cut using long, even strokes. Do not close the blades all the way. Open them up, and reposition them along the cutting line before cutting into a new section of foil. Cut into corners from both sides, rather than try to cut continuously around the corner.

You can easily cut thinner foils with a variety of tools. You can cut straight lines using either a craft knife or a rotary cutter with a straightedge, or a paper cutter. Cut decorative edges using pinking shears, decorative-edged paper scissors, or a decorative-edged rotary cutter. Specialty cutters commonly used in making scrapbooks, such as circle and oval cutters, also work for foil. Newly available shape cutters will quickly and easily allow you to cut multiples of a shape from foil, making them ideal for garland or wreath components, Christmas ornaments, or wall borders.

EMBOSSING

Embossing is one of the easiest and most versatile metalworking skills. Designs can be simple—freehand swirls, squiggles, dots, and lines—or elaborate representational sculptures. You can create simple textures using nothing but dots or scribbles. You can use line drawings, clip art, rubber stamp designs, and stencils as embossing patterns.

Because embossing is a technique that creates a raised or depressed pattern, you will need a tool to shape the metal foil. Tools for embossing include a dry ballpoint pen, a small wooden dowel shaped and blunted on the end, or metal styluses with ends of various shapes and sizes. Household items such as a dressmaker's tracing wheel, pasta crimper, or plastic silverware can be used to emboss patterns in foil. Embossing tools from other crafts, such as a paper embosser, work well on thinner foil. Crimpers or embossers with diamonds, hearts, dots, and other patterns are readily available. Look for these tools in the scrapbook or rubber stamp sections of craft stores.

To emboss, first place the metal foil on a padded work surface, such as an old phone book or magazine. To create raised embossing, place the foil with its wrong side up; to create depressed embossing, place the foil right side up. When creating raised embossing, reverse directional patterns, such as lettering, so that the pattern will read correctly on the right side of the foil. If you are working from a pattern, tape the pattern onto the foil or transfer the outline to the foil using carbon paper. Outline the entire design first, and then fill in the design elements. Remove the paper pattern after you have traced over all of the design lines. Using repetitive strokes to shape the foil without pressing so hard that you wear through the foil. Turn the foil over now and then to check the depth of the embossing. To further define embossed lines, create the opposite style of embossed line (raised or depressed) next to the original embossed lines. Smooth puffed areas with a spoon-shaped embossing tool or the eraser end of a pencil.

When using lighter-weight foils for items that will be used frequently, you need to support the embossing. To support the embossing, fill in the negative areas, or holes, on the wrong side of the foil using white glue, wax, or plaster. Allow the glue, wax, or plaster to completely cure, and then fasten the foil to the project.

Experiment with embossers, embossing tools, and techniques to add interest to foil projects and to personalize them. Add embossed lines to plain foil for a simple design, or outline a design to highlight it. Try embossing names, initials, or sayings onto foil projects to add a personal touch.

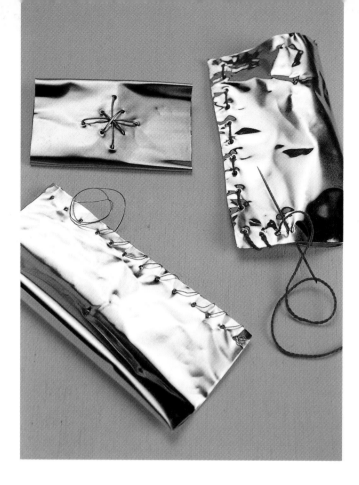

PUNCHING

You can punch metal foil using two basic techniques. The traditional method is to puncture the foil with an awl, nail, screwdriver, or metal punch. You can drive the metal punch through most foil with your hand, but for lower-gauge, or thicker, foil, use a hammer. Punched tin is created using the traditional method. Americana designs often incorporate punched tin, and it is a favorite material for making lamp shades because light will shine through the punched holes.

The second method for punching foil is to use a paper punch. With a paper punch, you can make holes of various shapes in the foil or remove shaped pieces of foil that you can then appliqué onto another surface. Use the paper punch in the same manner as when using it with paper. Punched-out shapes can be further embellished with embossing, beads, or paint treatments before appliquéing. Save all of your punched-out foil shapes to use as embellishments on other items, such as candles, stamped cards, journals, vases, or frames.

joining metal foil

The most desirable method to use when joining metal foil pieces depends on the project design and the amount of stress the joints or seams will be exposed to. Using two methods together can make a joint or seam more secure. For example, place a bead of adhesive on a fold line before folding the foil into place, or after gluing pieces together, stitch a wire across a seam.

FOLDING FOIL

Folding foil seams together is a temporary holding technique. You can also use this technique for joining foils that will not be exposed to stress. Make a simple fold by bringing the right-side edges of the foil together and bending ⅛" to ¼" (3 mm to 6 mm) of the foil edges to one side. To make a double-fold seam, first make a simple fold, and then fold and bend the foil edges one more time to the same side. A double-folded seam has no "raw" edges. If the folds will be permanent, smooth and seal them by rubbing them with the side of an embossing tool or small dowel.

STITCHING FOIL

Foil pieces may be joined mechanically with wire, thread, yarn, string, or ribbon using needlework techniques. Punch holes in the foil using the tool appropriate to the foil and diameter of stitching material. Common stitches include the running stitch, overcast stitch, and blanket stitch. Don't pull the stitching material so hard that you tear the foil.

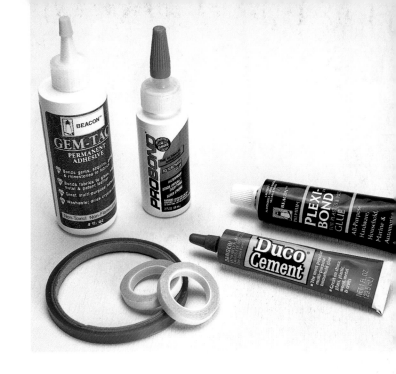

USING ADHESIVES

The properties of adhesives vary and can be adversely affected by extreme temperatures and humidity. If your project will be exposed to environmental extremes or will be placed under above-normal stress, you should test the adhesives under those conditions before making the project.

Some metal foil manufacturers produce double-sided tape or other forms of adhesives compatible with their product line. Check your foil packaging for recommendations. You can also check the manufacturer's Web site, many of which are listed on page 124, for further recommendations.

Double-sided tape produced by foil manufacturers, heavy-duty double-sided crafting tape, and all-purpose double-sided tape all work well on thinner foil. Tapes produced to hold glass and mirrors also work well on all foil. Apply the tape to one surface, leaving the backing paper or plastic in place. Carefully align the surfaces to be joined, and then peel back a little of the backing paper or plastic at a time while pressing the two surfaces together. Take your time when taping foil pieces together—some tapes are so sticky that you will not be able to reposition or adjust the pieces later. Some tapes take a few days to cure to their maximum strength.

A Xyron machine that laminates and applies adhesive at the same time works well with all but the heaviest foils. The Xyron machine is another tool commonly used in paper crafting and scrapbook making. You can use the Xyron machine for several purposes: to adhere two light-weight foil sheets together to make a heavier foil; to apply adhesive to the backs of foils that will be applied to other surfaces; to apply adhesive to backs of foils that will be cut or punched into smaller pieces, so you don't have to apply adhesive to each individual piece; and to laminate foils to protect them from weathering. Using this machine saves time and produces cleaner-looking projects.

Adhesives intended to be used on glass and jewelry work well on most foil. Do not use white craft glue or "instant" glue. The designers have listed the adhesives they used in the Resources section, pages 122 to 123. If the suggested adhesives are not available in your area, ask for a glass or metal adhesive at your local hardware or craft store, and test it on a small scrap of foil before you use it on your project.

applying surface treatments

PAINTING

Painting with the proper type of paint is a quick, versatile surface treatment for foil. Most spray, metal, and plastic paints can be used on metal foil. If you are in doubt about the paint you would like to use, test some on a scrap of foil by painting a small amount and allowing the paint to cure. Follow all of the paint manufacturer's instructions for preparation, application, and drying times.

You can use traditional painting techniques on metal foils. Brushwork, antiquing, glazing, and faux finishing can all be used to personalize and add dimension to projects.

USING METALLIC PASTES

Metallic pastes can greatly enhance embossed areas and can be used over antiquing or glazing techniques to add even more depth and interest. Lightly graze over the raised embossed areas with a fingertip or rag that has been dipped into the paste. Buff the paste with a soft rag to bring out the luster.

USING POWDERED PIGMENTS

Use fine mica pigments, sold in powder form, to add exciting accents to foil projects. Mica pigments are sold in a variety of colors, including dual-colors and interference colors that give off different hues, depending on the way light hits them. These pigments must be mixed into a medium that is compatible with the foil, such as PVA glue, candle-painting mediums, and glass and tile mediums. Mix the pigments into the mediums to a creamy consistency. Apply the mica pigment mixture with a paintbrush or sponge.

STAMPING

You can use rubber and foam stamps either as surface treatments or as patterns for embossing. Use the stamps with paints or dye inks that are compatible with metal foil. Try using rubber stamps with pigment inks and fine embossing powder on surfaces that won't be flexed for different effect.

CREATING PATINAS

Over time, untreated foils develop their own natural patina. Temperature, humidity, and exposure to salt air or pollution all affect the rate and outcome of a natural patina.

You can create a patina on steel foil by applying apple cider vinegar. Use straight apple cider vinegar on the steel foil, allowing it to puddles and run down the foil. You can also dab it on for a more subtle effect. Once you achieve the desired degree of rust, rinse the foil under tap water, allow it to dry, and then apply a clear acrylic sealer to prevent further rusting.

Chemical patinas instantly age untreated metal foils. Read the manufacturer's instructions carefully because some of these products emit noxious fumes. Check in craft stores and art supply stores to find a patina chemical for your type of foil and needs.

Liver of sulfur, found at art supply stores, is a common patina-creating chemical used on untreated copper. Dab it onto copper foil to create areas of purple, gray, blue, and black. Be sure to wear gloves and work in a well-ventilated area on a protected work surface. First clean the copper with rubbing alcohol, and then dilute 1 teaspoon of liver of sulfur in 4 cups of water. Dab the diluted mixture onto the copper using a rag or cotton balls. The copper will darken as it dries.

COLORING WITH HEAT

You can create an interesting finish on natural, untreated copper foil by heating it. Only use foil that is recommended for this technique by the manufacturer. Wear gloves and use tongs to handle the metal when using this technique because the copper gets very hot. Be sure to work in a well-ventilated space. Hold the copper with tongs in a gloved hand while you heat the bottom of the foil with a lighter or hold it over a stove burner. Once the foil is hot, it rapidly changes colors. Remove the foil from the heat source immediately once the color you desire appears.

USING PAINT PENS AND MARKERS

Because they vary greatly in their coverage and durability, test pens and markers on a scrap of foil before using them on a project. Most paint pens work well on foil, and many provide excellent coverage. Markers work best over painted surfaces or as temporary marking devices.

BEADING

Adhere microbeads or tiny marbles to foil to create a relatively easy and dramatic effect. Use heavy-duty double-sided tape, clear laminating adhesive, or metal-compatible glue to attach the beads. Apply the adhesive, place the project over some scrap paper, and then pour the beads over the adhesive. Press the beads into the adhesive, and pour any excess beads off onto the paper.

working with wire

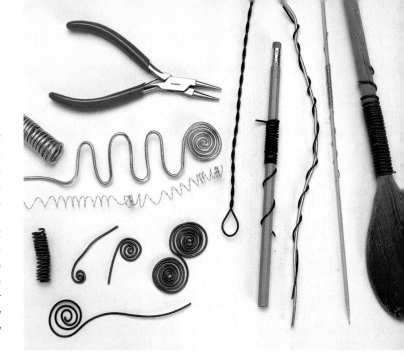

USING TOOLS FOR WIRE

You can make most of the projects in this book using simple tools—wire cutters or nail clippers, round-nose pliers, and wooden dowels or skewers. You can use nail clippers to cut thin copper wire, but you'll need to use wire cutters for thicker wire or for wire made from harder metals. Round-nose pliers make turning loops on the ends of wires, starting spirals, or twisting the ends of wires together quick and easy. Dowels, tool handles, pencils, and skewers can all be used to curl or coil wire.

If you'd like to advance your wire-working skills, you may want to acquire a few additional tools. A pair of side cutters allows you to trim wires closely and neatly. You can use channel pliers to straighten wire. Using a wire jig allows you to make the same pattern numerous times without tedious measuring. A power or hand drill greatly speeds the process of making twisted, multi-ply wires. Refer to page 124 to locate sources for these and many other wire-working tools.

CUTTING

Plastic-coated wire is safe and easy to cut, but other wires require a measure of caution. Because wire is made of metal, it has a tension that is released when it is severed, causing the wire ends to spring outward in random directions. In most instances, the larger the wire and the harder the base metal, the more it will spring out. When cutting wire, you should err on the side of caution and wear safety glasses and gloves. Hold onto either side of the wire that you are cutting to prevent it from springing in an unexpected direction.

TWISTING

Twisting wire gives the wire added size, strength, and texture. However, twisting creates tension in the wires, so work with caution. Don't overtwist. Wires will buckle and creep up and over the original twists when they are overtwisted. Wear safety equipment, such as safety glasses and gloves, when releasing twisted wire from a doorknob or other secured point.

You can use three basic methods to create a twisted, multi-ply wire: hand wrapping, twisting by hand around a dowel, and twisting with a drill. Hand wrapping is effective only for very light wires and produces an uneven, primitive look. Hand twisting around a dowel works for almost all wires and produces an even twist. Twisting with a drill is quick and easy, and produces an even, professional look. All of these methods require a length of wire at least three times the desired finished length.

To hand-wrap wire, hold the wires in one hand or place them in a tool, such as a clamp or a vise. Hold the opposite wire ends in the other hand, and twist and wind them around each other.

To hand-twist around a dowel, fold the wire in half, and place the center loop over a doorknob or other stable point. Wrap the loose wire ends around a sturdy dowel—at least ¾" (2 cm) in diameter—a couple times, making sure the wire is secure. Grasp both ends of the dowel and back up until the wire is taut between the dowel and the doorknob. Rotate the dowel to twist the wire, keeping the wire evenly taut. When you finish twisting the wire, remove the wire loop from the doorknob, and cut off the ends.

To twist wire with a drill, use the same process as you did for twisting wire around a dowel, with the only difference being that the loose wire ends are inserted into a drill chuck. Make sure the ends are secure in the chuck before operating the drill. Keep the wires taut and horizontal for the best results.

COILING

Wrapping wire around an object multiple times produces a coil. Coils can be decorative, functional, or both. After coiling the wire, you can separate or flatten the coils. You can also add another design element by threading beads onto wires before they are coiled. You can make coils in any size and in any shape. Use dowels, pencils, skewers, or any somewhat round object to make a coil. Coiling mandrels—tools made specifically for coiling—can be purchased at craft stores or from wire suppliers.

To make a coil, wrap the wire around the dowel or coiling tool, keeping the wraps tightly together. Wrap the wire to the desired length, and then trim the wire and slide the coil off the tool. To curl and kink wire, use the same procedure, but wrap the wire in a random, casual manner.

SPIRALING

Wire spirals are an interesting decorative element, but they can also be functional as holders. Spirals are also a good way to end wires because their ends are enclosed. Craft stores and wire suppliers offer many tools to make even, perfect spirals, but with practice, you can also make nice spirals by hand. Add some pizzazz to your project by making a triangular or square spiral.

To start a spiral, twist a tight loop at one end of the wire using round-nose or needle-nose pliers. Remember, the size and shape of this initial loop affects the size and shape of the final spiral. Rotate the wire around the initial loop using either your hands (for soft wire) or pliers (for harder, thicker wire). Square off the corners as you rotate the wire to form triangle or square spiral. Continue working the wire around in ever-increasing diameters, keeping the wire flat until the spiral reaches the desired size.

CHAPTER TWO

metal foil gifts

This chapter is a great introduction to the techniques of metal foil crafting. Most of the projects are small, so you can make multiple copies or sets quickly and easily. If you're looking for the perfect hostess gift, wine tags might be the solution. While making the wine tags, you'll learn how to do simple embossing and how to work with wire and glass beads. For the gardener, the herb tags and butterfly plant pokes make perfect gifts. Twisted and shaped wires accent both garden projects, adding decoration and stability to the designs. A journal is a welcome gift on many occasions, especially when it's decorated with one-of-a-kind adornments, like the copper dragonfly. Wrap any bottle with a metal foil label, add some wire and beads, and you have a beautiful gift, no matter what the bottle contains.

FESTIVE
bottle wraps

Dress up bottles and jars to use as gifts or decorative accents in the kitchen or bath. The large array of color for both foil and wire allows you to make a wrap to fit any decor. The flat surface of the wraps can easily be painted, beaded, stenciled, and embossed, adding even more versatility to this project.

MATERIALS	
• Bottle or jar • 1 sheet of foil in desired color • 3 yards (2.7 m) 22-gauge wire • Double-sided tape • Scissors	• Embossing tool • Measuring tape • Straightedge • Craft knife • 2 sizes of frosted glass beads for embellishment

step one

Measure the circumference of the bottle or jar by wrapping the measuring tape around the desired position for the wrap. Add 1" (2.5 cm) to this measurement to obtain the width of the wrap. The height of the wrap should fit the size and shape of the bottle or jar. The bottle wrap shown in this project is 4" (10.2 cm) high. Use a straightedge and craft knife to cut the foil to size.

step two

To create the top and bottom edges of the wrap, lay a straightedge on the wrong side of the foil, and fold at least ¼" (6 mm) of the foil over the straightedge. After you have created the top and bottom edges, decorate the wrap by embossing a design. Allow the paint to dry completely before continuing to the next step.

step three

Fold back ½" (1.3 cm) of foil on one of the short sides of the wrap. Apply double-sided tape along the top and bottom edges of the wrong side of the wrap. Peel off the paper backing of the tape and press the wrap to the bottle or jar, covering the unfolded short side with the folded side for a smooth finish.

step four

Coil and bead sections of wire as desired. Then wrap the beaded sections around the bottle or jar, securing the ends by twisting them together. Add additional bands of folded or crimped foil, adhering them to the wrap with double-sided tape.

variation

You can cover any bottle using the previous techniques. Vary the color of foil and beads, the twist of the wire, and the embossing with the bottle shape and contents to make a unique gift.

DANGLING wine glass charms

Have you ever noticed at parties how often people forget which glass is theirs? You can solve this problem by making and using these elegant stemware charms. The clips, made of plastic-coated wire, make these charms easy to remove and very durable. Embossed copper charms with glass bead accents are quick and easy to craft for a crowd, and a set makes a great hostess gift.

MATERIALS	• Medium-weight copper foil	• Awl
	• 18- and 22-gauge copper wire	• Round-nose pliers
	• Variety of glass beads	• Nail clippers or wire cutters
	• Embossing tool	• Patterns on page 114
	• Scissors	

step one

Copy the wine charm patterns from the back of the book (see page 114) or make your own shapes. Place the patterns on the copper foil, and use your embossing tool to trace around the patterns. Use the scissors to cut out the charms. Emboss the charms with outlines, squiggles, dots, or words, such as names of different types of wine.

step two

Pierce the top of each charm with an awl to create a hole in which to attach the beaded wire. Cut 6" to 8" (15 cm to 20 cm) of 22-gauge wire for each charm. Thread the 22-gauge wire through the hole, and wrap the wire back around itself to secure the charm to the wire. Add beads to the wire coil, or shape the wire into zigzags, leaving a 1" (2.5 cm) tail of wire. Refer to the photograph on page 25 for placement and design ideas.

step three

Cut a 6½" (17 cm) piece of 18-gauge wire for each charm. Bend small, tight loops on each end of the wire with the round-nose pliers. Fold each end of the wire back ¾" (2 cm) to make a hook shape. Shape the wire into a ring, hooking the folded ends around each other.

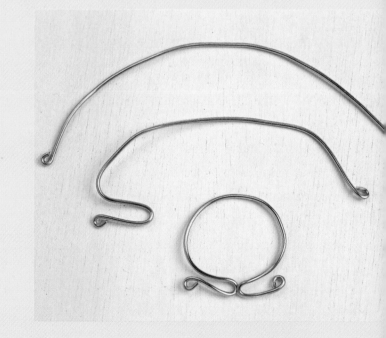

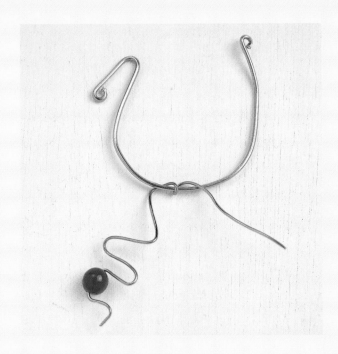

step four

Wrap the charm wire tail around the center of the wire clip a couple of times. Closely trim all 22-gauge wires. To attach to stemware, open clip by squeezing it or unhooking wire ends.

variation

Express your party theme with vivid foils and wires in vibrant colors. For a seashore or lake theme, emboss fish and shells onto foil. A garden-party theme is beautifully represented with flowers. Simple symbols, such as stars, moons, and hearts, can be dynamic when done with brilliant foils, wires, and beads. Try tracing a design motif from your invitations or linens onto the foil, then adding coordinating or contrasting beads and wire.

herb tags

Not sure which herb is sage and which is oregano? Plant tags can help novice gardeners

identify plants, mark dormant plants, and also provide a decorative accent. The folded

edges on these copper foil tags protect hands from cuts. The untreated surface of this foil

will develop a natural patina over time, only adding to the charm of these tags. You can

write the names of the herbs either freehand or using a computer font. The tags featured

in this project were created using the Lucinda Handwriting font.

<table>
<tr><td rowspan="2">MATERIALS</td><td>

• 2½" x 3" (6.5 cm x 7.5 cm) piece of copper tooling foil for each tag
• 18" (46 cm) 18-gauge copper-colored wire per tag
• Embossing tool
• Scissors

</td><td>

• Wire cutters
• Round-nose pliers
• Awl
• Patterns on page 115

</td></tr>
</table>

step one

Using the patterns on page 115, trace the larger oval onto the foil. Trace the smaller oval inside the larger oval. Use the scissors to cut the foil along the larger oval line.

step two

Write the names of the herbs on the patterns freehand, or choose your favorite font and print out the names from your computer. Then, lay the pattern or printout on the back of the small ovals, with the text facing the tag (so that you will be embossing the text in reverse). Use the embossing tool to write the plant name in the center of the small oval. Add some dots around the outline of the small oval.

step three

Using an awl, pierce the top center of the tag to create a hole in which to insert the wire. Then insert the wire, going from the back out to the front. Twist a tight loop in one end of the wire, and bend and shape the wire into a hook. Bend ½" (1.3 cm) from the loop, ¾" (2 cm) from the first bend, and then 1¼" (3 cm) from the second bend (see photograph at left).

variation

Cut a 2½" x 3" (6.3 cm x 7.5 cm) piece of medium-weight foil. Fold all edges in and over by folding the foil over the edge of a countertop or table and then pressing down the wrong side. Smooth the foil down with the side of the embossing tool. You can then emboss the plant name on foil and create the wire hook as in step 3.

BUTTERFLY
plant pokes

Want to add pizzazz to a potted plant or your garden? This foil and wire butterfly plant poke just might be the answer. Double layers of foil make this project attractive from both sides while adding sparkle and whimsy.

MATERIALS	
• Sheets of blue, pink, and lavender foil • 3 yards (2.7 m) 18-gauge black plastic-coated wire • Double-sided adhesive sheets, or a Xyron machine • Embossing tool	• Scissors • Wire cutters • Round-nose pliers • Drill • Patterns on page 116

step one

Use a drill to make 13" (33 cm) of twisted wire with the 18-gauge wire. For a longer poke, twist longer lengths of these wires or wrap these wires around a length of metal rod. Cut 8" (20 cm) of wire using the wire cutters, fold the wire in half, and then shape spirals on each wire end to create the butterfly's antennas.

step two

Apply the double-sided adhesive sheets to the wrong side of the blue, pink, and lavender foils. Cut the sheets in half, and then one of the halves in half again. Peel the paper backing off the half sheet of foil. Fold the half sheet, placing the wrong sides together, to make a double-sided sheet of foil. Smooth out any wrinkles or bumps.

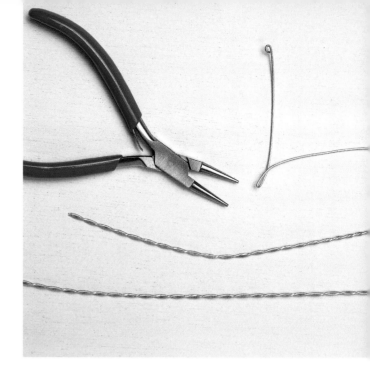

step three

Copy the butterfly pattern from the back of the book (see page 116). Place the wings pattern on the double-sided foil, and trace around the outline with the embossing tool. Use the scissors to cut out the butterfly shape. Place the body pattern (see page 116) on a contrasting color foil, and trace over the pattern lines with the embossing tool. Trace the wings spots onto the contrasting color foil. Cut out the body and wing spots. Remember to cut two bodies and two sets of wing spots so your butterfly will be completely finished on both sides.

step four

Place 1" (2.5 cm) of the folded end of the antenna wire on the foil head. Place the twisted wire under the antenna wire fold running down the length of the body. Peel the paper backing off the body, align the edges, and press the body down, covering the wires. Peel the paper backing off of the wings spots, and press them onto the wings.

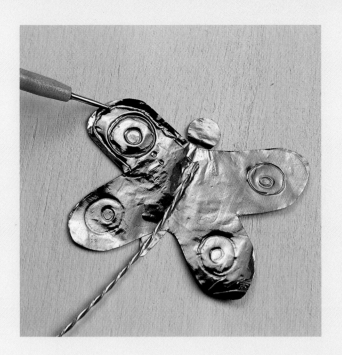

step five

Emboss around body and wing spots, adding as many details and lines as desired.

variation

Enlarge the basic pattern to make jumbo plant pokes or to make a series of large butterflies to decorate a wall, rattan basket, or wreath.

FOIL-EMBELLISHED
journal

Journaling is one of the fastest-growing pastimes, so why not do it with style? Use layers of handmade paper for the base to highlight the stamped, embossed, and treated foil. Add some accents of hammered wire shapes for that finishing touch.

MATERIALS

- 3½" x 4¾" (9 cm x 12 cm) natural-colored paper journal
- 4 coordinating sheets of handmade papers
- 3" (8 cm) square of lightweight, untreated copper foil
- 16" (41 cm) of 22-gauge copper wire
- 2" (5 cm) dragonfly rubber stamp
- Dye-based ink
- Decorative-edge scissors

- Glass adhesive
- Paper adhesive
- Tongs
- Candle or lighter
- Wire cutters
- Hammer
- Paper towel

step one

To create a soft edge on the handmade paper, first fold the paper at the desired dimension. Dampen the fold with water, and gently tear the sides of the paper apart. Tear a sheet of paper to a size that covers most of the front of the journal. Tear additional pieces of paper to create a collage over the cover. Arrange the papers as desired, and then glue them to the journal cover using the paper adhesive.

step two

Use a rubber stamp, such as the dragonfly stamp used on this project, and dye-based ink to create a design on the copper foil. Allow the ink to dry. Cut out the dragonfly with the decorative-edged scissors, leaving an uneven margin of copper around the design.

step three

To add depth and dimension to the dragonfly, hold the copper foil with tongs over the flame of a candle or lighter. The copper will discolor, based on the length of time it's heated and amount of heat that is used.

step four

Shape the copper wire randomly, using swirls and zigzags. Refer to the photograph (at left) for ideas. Place the wire on a hard surface, cover it with a paper towel, and hammer the wire flat. Then, glue the shaped wire and copper cutout to the journal using the glass adhesive.

variation

Cut a piece of copper smaller than the front of your album cover. Emboss lettering, and add details to the edges of the copper. Apply a patina solution to the copper, following the manufacturer's instructions. Glue the copper to the front of the album. For additional embellishment, cut the shanks off brass tacks with wire cutters, and glue the heads to the corners of the copper piece.

CHAPTER THREE

wall decorations

In this chapter, you'll find a project to fit any wall space and decorating style. Use the techniques in the faux tin tile mirror project to add a classic look to frames or to make an architectural accent for any room. Add a one-of-a-kind window treatment to any window with punched metal pieces joined with wire and beads. Make practical and beautiful wall pockets from a wide variety of metals, to hold anything from dried flowers to incoming mail. Sprinkle stars around the house in the form of garlands or wall hangings. Candle sconces and picture frames done in traditional or contemporary styles round out the chapter with even more techniques.

FAUX TIN TILE
framed mirror

Transform a framed mirror into the perfect wall accent. Silver-colored foil is embossed, then whitewashed to give it that vintage look. This same technique can be applied to many other foil-covered surfaces, such as picture frames, shelf edges, boxes, lamps, and light-switch plates.

MATERIALS	
• Framed mirror with at least a 2"-(5 cm) wide frame; featured frame is 9" x 15" (23 cm x 38 cm) • Silver-colored foil 4" (10 cm) larger on all sides of the framed mirror • Double-sided adhesive tape • White paint for plastic • Silver metallic paste	• Embossing tool • Straightedge • Scissors • Paintbrush • Ruler • Paper towel • Pattern on page 117

step one

Remove the mirror from the frame and any clips or staples from the back of the frame that held the mirror in place.

step two

Center the foil over the mirror frame, and rub the foil around all edges of the frame to make an outline of the outer and inner edges. Measure in 1" (2.5 cm) from all inner edges, and lightly mark these lines with an embossing tool and a straightedge. Using scissors, cut out the center of the foil up to the embossed lines. Make your cuts straight into each corner, up to the pressed inner outlines.

step three

Copy the small tile pattern on page 117. Measure or lay out the tile pattern between the pressed foil outlines. Place embossed dots between the tiles to aid in adjusting the tiles to fit. If your frame is slightly larger than the pattern, allow for more space between the dots and the tile pattern. If your frame is smaller than the pattern, place the tile patterns closer together, and place the dots only around the edges. Start embossing in one corner. Emboss all pattern lines, then add the dot edging as needed.

step four

Apply double-sided tape to the inner and outer foil edges. Center the foil on frame right side up. Fold the inner foil edges in and around the inside of the frame, and then press them to the back. Package-fold the outer edges around the outside of the frame, also bringing them around to the back. Press all of the edges down firmly. Rub the smooth side of the embossing tool over all of the corners to smooth and flatten them.

step five

Brush white paint over the entire frame, wiping off any excess paint with a paper towel. Allow the paint to dry, and then apply silver metallic paste to the raised embossed areas. Place mirror back into the frame.

variation

Use this same technique with a colored foil to fit any color scheme in your home. Embossed red foil buffed with gold metallic paste takes on the depth and richness of gold leaf. You can also try blue or green foils, using a silver or copper paste. Copper paste on blue or green foil will create a verdigris patina. Use a small amount of metallic paste at a time, adding and building to the desired depth of color. Avoid pressing too hard when buffing the metallic paste so that you don't flatten the embossed design.

SPARKLING
window valance

Emboss, punch, and paint metal to create this whimsical window treatment.
By punching metal sheets into circles and using simple embossing tools, you'll
transform a sunny window into a work of art. Apply glass paint for color, and
connect the circles with wire and beads. You'll find this project fast, fun, and easy.

<table>
<tr><td rowspan="2">MATERIALS</td><td>

• 32-gauge silver foil
• 18-gauge green and blue wire
• Glass paint, blue
• Glass paint surface cleaner
• Giant circle punch

</td><td>

• ¹⁄₁₆" (2 mm) hole punch
• Beads, aqua and clear
• Wire cutter
• Pliers
• Paintbrush

</td></tr>
</table>

step one

For a 26" (66 cm)-wide window, punch 32 silver foil circles using the giant punch. For a larger window, punch additional circles. Create raised embossed designs using an embossing pattern die placed randomly across the circles.

step two

Clean the front and back surfaces of each punched circle with the glass paint surface cleaner. Paint about one-half of the embossed design on each circle, using the glass paint. Allow one side to dry before painting the other.

step three

Use the ¹⁄₁₆" (2 mm) hole punch to punch a hole ⅛" (3 mm) in from the top and bottom edges of 24 of the circles. Punch a hole ⅛" (3 mm) from the top edge only of the remaining circles.

step four

Using the wire cutters, cut 16 pieces of wire, 2" to 3" (5 cm to 7.6 cm) each, from each color. Thread and center beads onto the wire, and loop each end of the wire using the pliers. Connect four circles to the wire-and-bead links. Attach the wire-and-bead links to curtain rings or loop them directly onto a curtain rod.

variation

Embossed flowers are joined with wire and glass-wrapped with silver adhesive foil. Add sparkle to any window with foil circles or other shapes punched from foil colors to complement your room. Hung over draperies or alone, foil valances of stars, hearts, or gem shapes are an unexpected, exciting accent.

RUSTIC CHARM
wall pocket

Whether this project is used to hold dried flowers or bills, its simple design and rustic style make it a welcome addition to any room. Simply apply apple cider vinegar to give the steel foil an aged look. To soften the look, try lacing the foil together with ribbon or yarn and painting the steel.

MATERIALS	
• 9" x 14" (23 cm x 36 cm) sheet of steel tooling foil • 9' (3 m) of 18-gauge black wire • Scissors • Awl • Clothespins	• Ruler or measuring tape • Apple cider vinegar • Paper towels • Clear acrylic sealer in matte or satin finish • Old phone book or magazines

step one

Cut the sheet of foil into two 8½" x 6½" (22 cm x 17 cm) pieces. Place the foil flat on a stack of paper towels, and either dab on apple cider vinegar for a light rusted look, or liberally pour it on, allowing it to puddle for more defined rusting. Depending on temperature and humidity, allow the vinegar to remain on the steel for 20 to 60 minutes. Rinse off the vinegar with plain water, and set the steel aside to dry.

step two

Spray two coats of clear acrylic sealer over the steel, following the manufacturer's instructions for application and drying time. By coating the steel, you will prevent further rusting and keep the rust particles from rubbing off.

step three

Stack the steel pieces together, matching all edges. Clamp the steel together every 4" (10 cm) or so with clothespins. Place the steel on an old phone book or stack of magazines, and use the awl to poke holes on three sides, about 1" (2.5 cm) apart. Cut a 6' (2 m) length of wire to lace the pocket together.

step four

Start lacing the wall pocket together by passing the wire through the top holes on one side from front to back. Pull all but 5" (13 cm) of wire through. Bring the wire back around to the front so that the wire wraps around the sides. Then poke the wire into the next set of holes. Repeat this process all the way around the pocket, being careful to not pull so hard on the wire that you rip the steel around the holes.

Wrap 2' to 3' (.6 m to .9 m) of wire around the leftover lacing wire, and bring the ends of both wires over to the top wire loop on the opposite side. Twist the wire to secure it and form the handle. Kink and shape all wire ends in designs of your choice. Shape the remaining wire, and wrap it around base of the wire handle.

variation

Make a versatile wall pocket by laminating two layers of thinner foil together. Roll the laminated foil into a cone-shaped pocket, and place it into a wire holder. Cut out some foil shapes, emboss them, and join them using one of the methods from the Basics chapter.

Cut two foil shapes, emboss them, and join them by folding. Hang the foil art with a wire strung with glass beads.

METALLIC GALAXY
ornaments

You'll think of dozens of ways to sprinkle stars around the house.

Use stars as ornaments on drawer pulls, lamp shades, and frames.

You can also hang them on their own. Wrap stars around candles,

planters, bottles, or jars. Why not make a series of brightly colored

stars to adorn the walls of a child's room?

MATERIALS	
• 12" (30 cm)-wide sheet of aluminum foil • 3' (1 m) of 22-gauge blue metallic wire • Embossing tool • Scissors • Awl • Round-nose pliers	• Wire cutters or nail clippers • Bamboo skewer • Small glass beads • 24-gauge brass wire • Silver-toned beads • Pattern on page 118

step one

Copy and enlarge the star patterns from page 118 by 125% to 200%. Trace the star outlines onto the foil using the embossing tool. Trace over the fold lines on the large and medium stars. Cut out the stars with the scissors.

step two

Emboss the sides of the large star using the freehand flower guide on the star pattern. Emboss the smallest stars with scribbles and repeated outlines.

step three

Heavily emboss the fold lines on the large and medium stars. Gently fold the large and medium stars by squeezing the sides of each fold line, pushing the star into a 3-D shape.

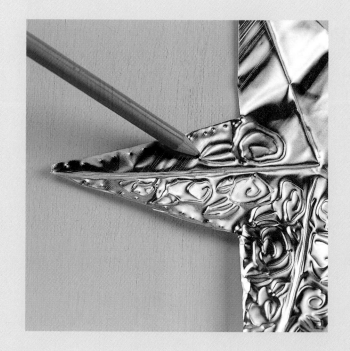

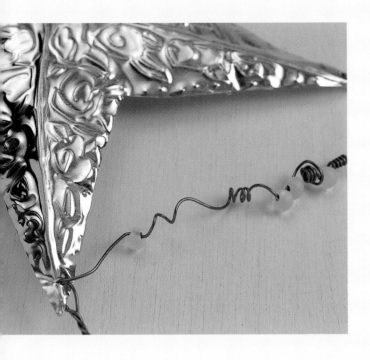

step four

Use the awl to poke a hole in one point of the large star. Thread 5" (13 cm) of the 22-gauge blue wire through the hole. Then fold the wire in half and hand-twist it.

step five

Form the twisted wire into a loop, and wrap the wire around the base of the wire next to the star. Carefully trim the wire ends using the wire cutters.

step six

Thread beads randomly onto 4" to 12" (10 cm to 31 cm)-long pieces of wire, twisting tight loops on the ends of the wire to secure the beads. Curl the wire between the beads by wrapping it around a bamboo skewer. Wrap the beaded wires around a wire hanger, and suspend one strand from a star's bottom point.

variation

Poke holes in the opposite points on all of the smaller stars. When assembling the garland, alternate star sizes and metal colors. Use a curled wire piece to join each star, adding one more curl on the end from which to hang the garland, or through which you can loop the end star. Thread two to five silver beads onto a 12" to 18" (31 cm to 46 cm) length of brass wire. Curl the centers of the wires by wrapping them around a bamboo skewer, leaving 2" to 3" (5 cm to 8 cm) uncurled on each end. Insert the wire ends through the holes in the star points, and wrap the wire around star point. Finally, curl the wire ends using a skewer.

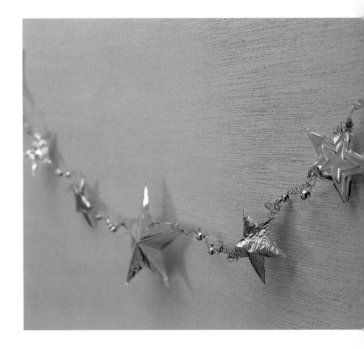

RED
heart sconce

Set a romantic mood with this lovely heart candle sconce. Armature wire makes an easy- to-form base. The textured background reflects the flickering candle, and the beads add the final touch of sparkle.

MATERIALS	• 9" x 24" (23 cm x 61 cm) red foil • 48" (122 cm) of 14-gauge armature wire • 26-gauge silver wire • Red E beads • Double-sided tape	• Glass votive with small candle • Texture sheet • Brayer (ink roller) • Needle-nose pliers • Scissors

step one

You can easily shape armature wire by hand. To start the sconce's frame, fold the wire in half. Then pull the ends in opposite directions to form a small hanging loop, about ½" (1.3 cm) in diameter. With the loop pointing down and the two ends pointing up, curve the ends to form a flat heart shape, about 9" (23 cm) across. Twist the wires together at the bottom of the heart to secure them. Shape the ends of the wire around your glass votive.

step two

Using the outline of the wire heart frame as a pattern, trace the heart shape onto two pieces of the red foil, extending the heart pattern 1½" (3.8 cm) on all sides. Cut out the red foil hearts with the scissors.

step three

Emboss one piece of foil by placing it over any object with texture, such as a texture sheet. Rub the foil firmly over the texture sheet using either a brayer or your finger wrapped in a soft cloth. The sheet shown in the photograph at left was made from a stamped sheet of polymer clay that was baked according to the manufacturer's instructions. Heavy laces, leaves, wire mesh, jewelry, or carved wooden pieces make excellent background textures.

step four

On the silver side of one heart piece, place two rows of double-sided tape 1½" (3.8 cm) and 2" (5 cm) in from the edges. Center the flat side of the wire heart frame on the silver side, and make a small slit in the foil for the hanging loop. Peel the paper backing off of the row of double-sided tape that is 1½" (3.8 cm) from the edge.

step five

Cut ½" (1.3 cm)-wide tabs all the way around the heart, up to the edge of the frame. Fold the tabs around the wire frame, down onto the tape. Remove the paper backing from the second row of tape. Center the textured foil heart, red side up, over the front of the frame, and press it down firmly over the tape. Cut tabs in the same manner along the heart outline. Use needle-nose pliers to curl the tabs.

step six

Thread E beads onto the wire, and wrap the beaded wire around the part of the frame that will hold the votive. Insert the votive and candle.

variation

Wrap embossed copper foil around a block of wood. Drill a hole through the copper, and insert a twisted wire candleholder.

FUNKY-FOOTED
frame

Add funky polymer clay feet to a foil frame to get an outstandingly unique way to display a favorite photo. An acrylic frame forms the base, making this an easy, fun, and functional project.

MATERIALS

- 9" x 12" (23 cm x 31 cm) red foil
- Metallic red polymer clay
- 4" x 6" (10 cm x 15 cm) acrylic frame
- Double-sided tape or Xyron machine with adhesive-only cartridge
- Heavy-duty glue

- Texture sheet
- 5" x 7" (13 cm x 18 cm) piece of foam core
- Craft knife
- Brayer (ink roller)
- Scissors

step one

Use a craft knife with a sharp blade to cut a 2½" to 3" (6 cm to 8 cm) opening in the center of the foam core. You can adjust the inside opening to fit your photograph.

step two

Add texture to the foil by embossing a random pattern or by placing the foil over any textured surface (such as heavy lace, wire mesh, carved wood, or images stamped into clay) and running a brayer over the foil or rubbing the foil with your finger wrapped in a soft cloth. You can also texture foil by tapping a pencil eraser or the end of a stylus repeatedly over the entire surface.

step three

Trim the foil to 6" x 7" (15 cm x 18 cm). With the scissors, cut eight 2" x ½" (5 cm x 1.3 cm) pieces of foil from the remaining foil. Apply adhesive to the small foil strips, and press them into or around the outside and inside corners on the foam core frame. Smooth the foil down tightly to the foam core.

step four

Center the foam core frame on the silver side of the 6" x 7" (15 cm x 18 cm) piece of foil. Apply strips of double-sided tape first around the outer edges of the foam core frame and then the inner edges. Remove the paper backing from the tape one side at a time. Then fold the foil up over the edge, and press it down into the tape. Remove the paper backing from tape around the opening. Cut an X shape into the opening, and fold each side around to the back. Using the heavy-duty glue, affix the back of the foil frame to the front of the acrylic frame.

step five

To make the clay "feet," condition the polymer clay, and shape it into a ½" (1.3 cm)-diameter roll. Cut two 2" (5 cm) pieces. Cut each of these pieces in half lengthwise to make four pieces. Taper and shape the end of each piece, referring to the photograph at left as a guide. Bake the clay according to the manufacturer's instructions. Once the clay has cooled, glue the "feet" to the acrylic frame, making sure the frame will stand upright.

variation

You can enhance embossed and textured foils by using paints and markers. Dents in the foil can be filled with paint and details outlined with markers. Add twisted wire hangers or stands of wire to further personalize a frame.

CHAPTER FOUR

all around the house

Metal foil is a versatile medium, easily transformed into a wide variety of decorative and functional items. In this chapter, you'll learn many ways to use and adapt metal foil to enhance every room in your home. Display flowers easily and uniquely with an embossed metal foil holder, custom fit to your container. With the Moroccan-style vase, you'll learn how to antique foil and how to add colored foil insets and mirrors. You'll also learn to make a celestial-style mobile to add sparkle and whimsy to any space. Cover lamp shades with metal foil to light up a room—even when the lamp is off. You can either cover the shade completely or appliqué shapes onto the shades to match any decor. A copper lantern with a special heat treatment finish makes a glowing accent in any room, but it's also the perfect addition to any outdoor space. Weave and sculpt metal foil to make a decorative box to hold your treasures or to just show off your artistic skills. The flower-embellished shower curtain gives further proof that metal foil can go almost anywhere.

FOIL-COVERED
flower holder

Short-stemmed flowers like pansies are now easy to display. Cover a glass container with punched and embossed foil to hold those fragile stems upright. Choose a color for your foil and beads that complements the flowers, your decor, or the season. Any glass or acrylic container can be adapted to this design by tracing the outline of the opening onto the center of a sheet of foil, and cutting a design to fall down the sides of the container.

MATERIALS		
	• 3" (8 cm) square glass votive	• Metal straightedge
	• 8" (20 cm) square of medium weight foil	• Round-nose pliers
	• Four glass beads	• Wire cutters
	• 24" (61 cm) of 22-gauge silver wire	• Scissors
	• Self-adhesive silver tape	• Bamboo skewer
	• ¼" (6 mm) hole punch	• Pencil
	• Craft knife	• Paper
	• Embossing tool	• Pattern on page 119

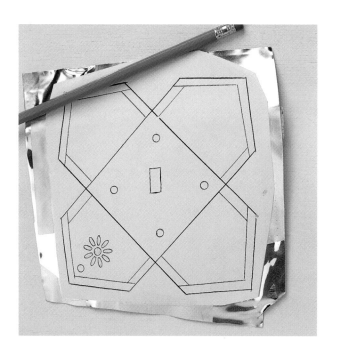

step one

From the foil, cut a square that is large enough to accommodate the top and sides of your vase. Cut a triangle out of the center of each edge, and fold the edges of each flap to make neat presentation. (See the photograph on page 69 for details.)

step two

For each flap, emboss around the outer edges, and add a flower design using the embossing tool. Emboss dots between the embossed outlines. Use scissors to cut out the shape.

step three

Using the hole punch, punch holes in the foil where indicated on the pattern. Cut a slot in the center of the foil using a craft knife. Then apply strips of self-adhesive silver tape to all sides of the center slot.

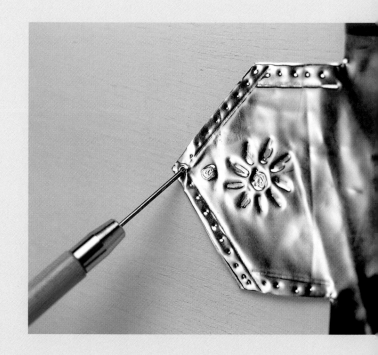

step four

Cut 6" (15 cm) of wire for each bead using the wire cutters. Thread the wire through each bead, twisting a small spiral at the base of the bead. Wind the wire around a bamboo skewer three times at the top of the bead. Thread the wire through a hole on the side points beneath the flowers, and twist the wire at the top of the bead to secure it.

step five

Fold the sides of the foil over the top of the glass votive, rolling the side of the embossing tool over the corners to smooth them.

variation

Make a paper pattern to fit your vase. Trace around the top of a round vase to get the dimensions of the opening, and then trace a circle 2" to 3" (5 cm to 8 cm) larger than the opening's dimensions. Fold the paper pattern into eighths, and trim triangle-shaped rays out from the opening dimension line. Trace and cut two copies of this pattern from light green foil. Emboss vein lines down each triangle, and stack the collars on top of each other, staggering the rays. Poke three to five holes in the center of each piece. Place the collars on the vase pressing the first one down, snug up against the vase.

MOROCCAN
mosaic vase

Want to add some ethnic flair to a room? Why not create this foil-and-mirror-mosaic vase for an exotic touch. The mosaic effect is created using only colored foils and mirrors, mounted to a layer of embossed foil. You can alter the color combinations to suit your room. When you've finished your vase, why not start on another for a gift?

MATERIALS	
• Square vase, 9" (23 cm) high with the sides tapering from 5½" to 3¼" (14 cm to 8 cm) • Silver-colored foil, 11" x 32½" (28 cm x 83 cm) • 5" (13 cm) squares of red, purple, and gold foils • Twenty ¾" (19 mm) mirror tiles • Eight 1" (3 cm) mirror tiles • Black Paint for Plastic • Mirror adhesive	• Double-sided tape • Embossing tool • Handheld diamond embosser (commonly sold for scrap booking and other paper crafts) • Paintbrush • Paper towels • Scissors • Xyron machine with adhesive-only cartridge

step one

Align one end of the foil up to the side of the vase, positioning the foil so that there is a ½" (1.3 cm) overhang on the sides and a 1" (2.5 cm) overhang at the top and bottom. Press the foil around the sides of the vase firmly enough to leave an impression of all sides. Trim the pressed foil from the rest of the foil. Cut three more identical pieces, and center them to the sides of the vase. Press them firmly to all edges of the vase to mark the sides. Cut a 3" to 4" (8 cm to 10 cm) square from the remaining foil, and set it aside.

step two

Fold all of the pressed foil outlines to the wrong side of the foil. Insert the foil into a handheld embosser, keeping the foil centered in the embosser while you turn the handle. If the foil pieces are wider than the handheld embosser, fold the foil down the center with wrong sides together. Run the colored foils through the embosser to imprint them.

step three

Adhere the side foil pieces to opposite sides of the vase, wrapping the edges over the corners and onto the adjacent sides. Apply strips of double-sided tape down the sides of the vase, ¼" (6 mm) in from the edges on the adjacent vase sides. Center the foil on the vase sides. Then remove the paper backing from the tape, and press the foil onto it. Trim off any excess foil along the sides.

steps four through ten

4. Package-fold the bottom edge of the foil. Apply a strip of double-sided tape to the inside of the vase. Miter the top corners of the foil, then press the mitered corners onto the tape.

5. Position the foil side pieces on the remaining two sides of the vase. Crease the foil along the sides, top, and bottom, and trim 1¼" (3 cm) from the crease. Apply strips of double-sided tape down the sides of the vase (on the side you'll be covering). Remove the paper backing one side at a time, and center the foil over the tape and press down firmly. Finish the top and bottom in the same manner that you did in the previous step.

6. Hem all sides of the foil square by folding all of the edges to the wrong side. Apply double-sided tape to all sides, and press a foil square onto the bottom of the vase.

7. Brush black Paint for Plastic over the entire vase, wiping off any excess with a paper towel. Allow the paint to dry.

8. To adhere the colored foil embellishments, you can either run the colored foil through a Xyron machine or place rows of double-sided tape or glue to the backs of the colored foil.

9. Cut the colored foil into small- and medium-sized diamonds using the embossing lines to guide you. Remove the paper backing, and press the colored foils onto the vase to create evenly balanced patterns. Refer to the photograph on page 73 for ideas. Outline the edges on all of the colored foil diamonds using the round end of the embossing tool.

10. Glue mirror tiles to the sides of the vase to highlight and complete the mosaic patterns.

variation

Cover the sides of a vase with a colored foil. Cut diamond shapes from a contrasting foil color. Emboss the diamonds with a pattern or an outline. Glue wood, foam, metal, or resin shapes to the foil diamonds.

STARS AND MOON
mobile

Give them the moon and stars! Punched and embossed foil shapes will shimmer when suspended from wires studded with crystal beads. The aluminum wire armature is easily shaped, and the punched foil shapes are quickly embossed, making this a great afternoon project.

MATERIALS	
• Sheets of blue and silver foils • 30" (76 cm) of 14-gauge aluminum armature wire • 26-gauge silver wire • Crystal E beads • 1¾" (4 cm) and ⅜" (1 cm) star-shaped punches • 1¼" (3 cm) moon-shaped punch	• Sheet adhesive or Xyron machine with adhesive-only cartridge • Embossing tool • Wire cutters • Round-nose pliers • Awl • Bamboo skewer

step one

Using the wire cutters, cut two 9" (23 cm) pieces of armature wire. Form spirals on opposite ends of one piece of wire, and make a curve in the center. (Refer to the photograph at left.) For the other wire, form spirals facing each other. Cut two 6" (15 cm) lengths of armature wire, and form spirals facing each other on these wires.

step two

Apply sheet adhesive to half of each blue and silver foil sheet. Remove the paper backing from the adhesive sheet, and fold the sheet in half, wrong sides together, to make a double-sided foil sheet.

step three

Punch four large stars from the blue double-sided sheet. Punch five moons and six small stars from the silver double-sided sheet. Emboss the large star and the moon outlines using the embossing tool. Then use the awl to poke holes in all punched pieces.

step four

Cut four 15" (38 cm) and two 20" (51 cm) lengths of 26-gauge silver wire. Wire the moons onto the ends of the two 20" (51 cm) lengths and two of the 15" (38 cm) lengths of wire by inserting the wire through the holes you made with the awl and looping the wire to wrap around itself.

step five

Place large stars on the ends of the remaining 15" (38 cm) wires and on two of the 20" (51 cm) wires with moons on the ends. Randomly add beads and punched stars to the wires. Curl the wires here and there by wrapping them around the bamboo skewer.

step six

Attach the adorned wires to the armature wires. Attach one of the 15" (38 cm) moon wires to the center of the 9" (23 cm) facing-spiral wire by wrapping the wire tail around the center of the armature wire. Attach a 15" (38 cm) blue star wire to the spiral ends of the same 9" (23 cm) opposing spiral wire. Leave a 1½" (4 cm) gap between the blue star wire and the moon wire. Wrap the blue star wire around the center of a 6" (15 cm) facing-spiral wire.

step seven

Wrap a 20" (51 cm) wire to one end of the 6" (15 cm) facing-spiral wire with a 15" (38 cm) moon wire on the opposite side. Hook the 9" (23 cm) wire with spirals and a center curve around the center of the other 9" (23 cm) wire to create a hanger for the mobile. Adjust and arrange wires to balance the mobile.

variation

Trace the top of a box onto foil to measure a piece of foil the right size. Emboss a sun or moon face on the foil. Paint the box and lid silver. Glue the embossed foil onto the box lid, and antique the foil and painted box with thinned black paint.

METALLIC
lamp shade

Revamp and recycle an old lamp shade, or dress up a new one, with metal foil accents. Lamp shades are available with patterns or with an adhesive already applied to them, which make this a quick decorating project. Why not make a frame and box to match?

MATERIALS	
• Lamp shade • Purple foil on a roll (The roll gives the extra length required.) • 1 sheet each of teal and lavender foil • Double-sided tape • Craft knife and straightedge or paper cutter (optional)	• Scissors • Large piece of paper, such as newspaper • Pencil • Xyron machine with adhesive-only cartridge (optional)

step one

Make a pattern for your lamp shade if it does not come with one. Lay the seam of the shade on the edge of a large piece of paper, such as a newspaper. Roll the shade across the paper while you hold a pencil next to the lower edge. Repeat this process for the top edge. Cut out the pattern with the scissors, adding ½" (1.3 cm) to all sides.

step two

Trace the outline of the paper pattern onto the purple foil, and then cut it out. Apply two rows of double-sided tape over the shade's seam.

step three

Remove the backing paper from one of the strips of tape. Center one end of the purple foil over the tape, and press down firmly. Roll the foil around the shade, and peel off the second strip's paper backing, pressing the other end of the foil to the shade.

step four

You can attach the colored foils to the lamp shade in one of two ways:

a. Cut teal and lavender foil sheets in half.

b. Run the foil sheets through the Xyron machine.

c. Cut both foils into ½" (1.3 cm)-wide strips using a paper cutter or a straightedge and a craft knife.

OR

a. Cut four ½" (1.3 cm)-wide teal strips and ten ½" (1.3 cm)-wide lavender strips.

b. Apply double-sided tape to the backs of all foil strips.

c. Evenly space four teal strips diagonally across the shade and attach. Apply four lavender strips between the teal strips and running diagonally the opposite direction.

d. Trim all the foils evenly at the top and bottom of the shade.

step five

Press the lavender strips around the top and bottom edges so that half of the strip overhangs the shade. (You'll need two strips on the bottom of the shade.) Clip the foil overhanging the shade every ¼" (6 mm), and fold the edges down. Apply lavender strips around the inside top and bottom of the shade, overlapping the clipped foil edges. Smooth all foil down snugly to the shade and to each other by rubbing it with a smooth tool handle.

variation

Weave multiple colors of foil together on a lamp shade for added texture. You can also emboss and antique the foil lamp shade cover and add a shaped wire trim.

COPPER GLOW
lantern

Light up the night with a perfect patio lantern with pinecone, leaf, and sunflower motifs. A quick and easy heating technique transforms the color of the untreated copper foil right in front of your eyes. Make these lanterns in various sizes, shapes, and motifs to vary with the seasons or your decor.

MATERIALS	
• 9" x 12" (23 cm x 30 cm) copper foil • Craft knife • Awl • Needle-nose pliers	• Stylus • Scissors • Heat gun • Patterns on pages 120 and 121

step one

Using the scissors, cut the copper foil into two pieces, 9"x 6" (23 cm x 15 cm) and 6" x 5" (15 cm x 13 cm). Using the stylus, score a line down the center of the larger piece to divide it into 4¼" x 6" (11 cm x 15 cm) sides.

step two

Tape copies of the pinecone and leaf patterns on pages 120 and 121 side by side onto 9" x 6" (23 cm x 15 cm) pieces of foil. Use a stylus to transfer all pattern lines onto the foil, and remove the paper patterns. Use an awl to punch holes where indicated by the dots on the pattern. Use a craft knife to cut along the solid pattern lines. Emboss the backside of the cut areas with the stylus to give them more dimension.

step three

Make a simple folded ⅛" (3 mm) hem along the top and bottom edges of the foil.

step four

To use the heat gun, place the copper on a heatproof surface, and hold the heat gun over the area you want to color. Use a scrap of foil as a mask to isolate areas you don't want to be colored.

step five

Double-fold the two pieces of foil together. Fold the larger piece of foil on the scored centerline. Double-fold the last two sides together to complete a triangular ring.

variation

Emboss and cut only flowers in the lantern for a spring-like atmosphere.

EMBOSSED
table box

Add an artful touch to any table with this woven foil box. Store small treasures inside the box, or simply enjoy the glimmering beauty of the 3-D dragonfly that adorns the lid. You can make more dragonflies to clip on curtains, place on vases, or lay beside the box as sculptures.

MATERIALS	• 4" x 9¼" (10 cm x 23 cm) pieces of gold, copper, green, and violet foil • Cigar box with sliding lid • Four ½" (1.3 cm) square wooden blocks for legs • ½" (1.3 cm) round wooden knob • Five ½" (1.3 cm) wood screws • Pearl paints in violet and turquoise • Gold metallic pastes (one light, one dark) • Double-sided tape	• Glass bead • Copper thread • Rotary cutter • Scissors • 1" (2.5 cm) and #6 paintbrushes • Fine-grit sandpaper • Clean, soft cloth • Power drill • Small dowel

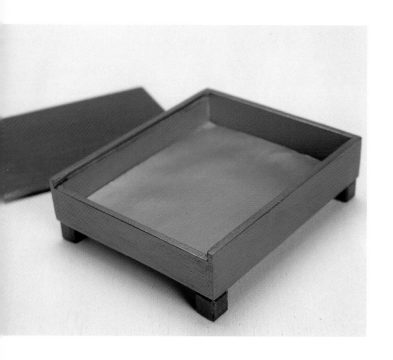

step one

Sand the cigar box smooth using the fine-grit sandpaper. Use a clean, soft cloth to apply the dark gold metallic paste to the wooden knob and the underside and top edges of the box. Buff the metallic paste until shiny. (The paste dries instantly, so you don't have to wait after applying it to buff it.) Apply the light gold metallic paste to the sides of the box using the same procedure.

step two

Paint the wooden blocks and underside of the lid pearl violet, and set it aside. Paint the inside of the box pearl turquoise. Allow all paints to dry.

step three

Attach the legs to the bottom corners of the box using the screws. Keep in mind that it will be easier to do this if you predrill the holes.

step four

Use the rotary cutter to cut seven ½" x 9¼" (1.3 cm x 23 cm) strips from each color of foil. Apply double-sided tape around the edges of the lid. Arrange the colored foil strips in a pleasing arranging, and adhere them to the tape on one side of the lid. Weave strips of the colored foils across the first strips in an over-under pattern. Press the ends of the foil onto the tape on all sides. Trim off any excess foil with scissors.

step five

Attach the knob to the lid with the remaining screw.

step six

To make the dragonfly ornament, cut three differently colored foil strips 4" (10 cm) long and link them together in a chain. Use double-sided tape to secure the ends and adhere the chains to the box. Cut five strips of foil, each 2" (5 cm) long, and curl them tightly around a small dowel. Tape the ends of the curled foil under the center link of the dragonfly.

step seven

Embellish the knob with copper thread and a glass bead.

variation

Follow the instructions above for the companion book, placing the woven strips at a diagonal. The diva embellishment was created with Friendly Plastic.

FLOWER-POWER
shower curtain

Create this mod flower-power shower curtain with punched foil and colorful wire. Recycle or update an old shower curtain, or buy a new one. In an hour, you'll have a curtain full of blooms. The flowers are attached with hook-and-loop strips so they can be removed when the shower curtain needs cleaning.

MATERIALS	
• Aluminum foil	• 5" (13 cm) of hook-and-loop strips
• White shower curtain	• Wire cutters
• 22- and 18-gauge silver wire	• Pliers
• Giant flower punch	• Embossing tool
• Fabric and gem glue	• Scissors

step one

Use the giant flower punch to create 20 foil flowers. Create raised embossed petal shapes on each flower using the embossing tool.

step two

Using pliers and 18-gauge silver wire, make 20 spirals, 5½" (14 cm) in diameter. Glue the spirals to the centers of the foil flowers using gem glue.

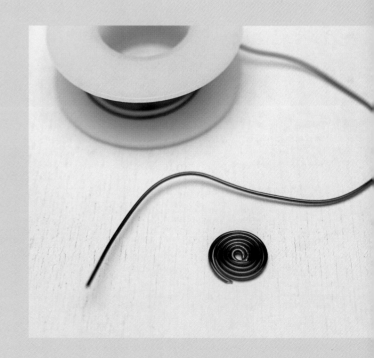

step three

Using the wire cutters, cut 20 pieces of 22-gauge wire, each 20" (51 cm) long. Form four or five 4" (10 cm) loops that resemble petals. Secure the center of the loops by wrapping one end of the wire around them, and trimming off the excess wire. Spread the loops apart to form petals.

step four

Cut twenty 1" (2.5 cm) pieces of hook-and-loop strip. Glue the wire petal shapes to the center of one side of the hook-and-loop strip with fabric adhesive. Glue the foil flower over the wire petals using gem glue. Allow all glue to dry.

step five

Glue the other side of hook-and-loop strip to the shower curtain using fabric glue, spacing flowers in staggered rows, about 11" (28 cm) apart and 8" (20 cm) in from all edges.

variation

You can appliqué punched foil designs to most surfaces to decorate ordinary objects. Adding an extended wire loop to the metal foil flowers used to embellish the shower curtain makes an excellent curtain tieback. Tie a room together with a foil motif by placing them on objects throughout the room.

CHAPTER FIVE

gallery

This Metal Foil Crafts Gallery contains works from a number of artists who specialize in metalworking, as well as those working in a wide variety of media. The designs in this chapter further illustrate the versatility and beauty of metal foil, as well as the imagination and skill of the artists. Let this chapter inspire you to explore and experiment with metal foil. Please see Contributing Artists on pages 125 and 126 for additional information about the artists.

Artist: Beth Wheeler

ANTIQUED COPPER
mantel clock

Give a traditional clock a vintage look by adding a softly antiqued copper finish. Instead of hunting through antique stores for that perfect mantle piece, make your own in an afternoon.

MATERIALS	
• Small mantel clock • Gold-colored foil • Double-sided tape • Scroll border stencil • Embossing tool • Dimensional Magic	• Light glaze medium • Soft beige acrylic paint • Stiff paintbrush • Mouse pad • Copper metallic paste • Scissors

1. Cut a piece of gold foil that is ½" (1.3 cm) larger on all sides than the top of the clock. Cut another piece larger all around than the front of the clock.

2. Place the foil pieces on the mouse pad, and lay the scroll border stencil on top. Outline the motifs through the stencil. Then turn the foil over, and emboss the motifs on right side of the foil using the embossing tool. Fill the embossing indentations with Dimensional Magic, and allow it to dry completely.

3. Mount the foil pieces on the top and front of the clock with the double-sided tape. Fold ½" (1.3 cm) of the foil under to create a simple, clean fold.

4. Mix the glaze medium and soft beige acrylic paint in equal amounts. Apply this mixture to all clock surfaces with a stiff, dry paintbrush. Allow the paint to dry completely.

5. Highlight any embossed areas with copper metallic paste.

Artist: Madeline Arendt

MINIATURE
book necklaces

Show off those darling baby pictures or keep special mementos close to your heart with one of these book necklaces. Vary the cords and beads on the necklaces to coordinate with any outfit.

MATERIALS	
• Copper foil • Double-sided tape • Foil leaves • Delta Paint Jewels • Rubber stamp • Beads • Chipboard	• Scrapbook paper in your choice of color for inner pages • Glue (for paper) • Scissors • Craft knife • Cording

1. Using the scissors, cut the chipboard to size for the front and back of the book. Cut a piece of copper foil that is 1" (2.5 cm) larger all the way around than the chipboard covers. Stamp the covers, and add the foil leaves for decoration.

2. Paint the stamped designs using the Paint Jewels.

3. Tape the foil to the outside surface of the chipboard covers with double-sided tape. Cut the inner chipboard covers slightly smaller than the outer covers, and cover them with foil. Add the inner book pages.

4. Glue the book together, adding some cording and beads for a personal touch.

Artist: Madeline Arendt

RUSTED TREE

mirror

Reflect your love of nature with this tree-border mirror. This versatile design, with its rich copper hue, makes a perfect accent in a den or library.

MATERIALS

- Copper foil
- Wooden frame
- Tree border stencil
- Alcohol-based inks
- Clear fixative

- Decorative edged scissors
- Embossing tool
- Stylus
- Metal punch
- Brass tacks

1. Use the decorative-edged scissors to cut the copper foil into strips. Size the strips so that they will fit over the mirror frame.

2. Place the stencil on the copper strips, and trace around the design with the small end of an embossing tool. Remove the stencil, and retrace the design using more pressure. Turn the copper strips over, and press inside the design to add texture.

3. Paint the embossed trees with alcohol-based inks. When you have finished painting, spray the strips with a clear fixative.

4. Attach copper strips to frame with brass tacks.

Artist: Kelley R. Taylor

EMBOSSED
iron frame

Elegant simplicity describes this art piece—classic styling at its best. You can find deep frames or shadow box frames in craft shops or in art supply stores.

MATERIALS	
• Shadow box frame with mat • Aluminum foil • Rust kit	• Scissors • Embossing tool • Glass adhesive

1. Trace a shape onto the foil. Cut out the shape with the scissors, and emboss it to your liking using the embossing tool.

2. Rust the piece, following the rust kit manufacturer's instructions.

3. Glue the rusted foil to the center of the shadow box frame mat using glass adhesive. Then insert it into frame.

Artist: Kelly R. Taylor

WOVEN
mirror

Three metal hues work together in harmony to create both interest and balance on this project.

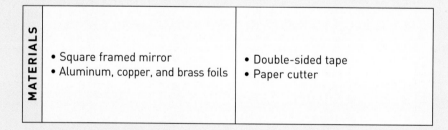

MATERIALS

- Square framed mirror
- Aluminum, copper, and brass foils
- Double-sided tape
- Paper cutter

1. Remove the mirror from the frame.

2. Use a paper cutter to cut all foils into 1" (2.5 cm)-wide strips, at least 4" (10 cm) longer than the width of the frame. Make simple folds ¼" (6 mm) in on all sides.

3. Place a strip of double-sided tape across one side of the back of the frame. Press the strips side by side onto the tape. Then, flip the strips over to the right side of the frame.

Weave the foil strips over and under through the first group of strips using double-sided tape to secure them to the backside. Cover the entire frame in this manner.

4. Adhere all of the remaining foil strips to the back of the frame with double-sided tape.

5. Place the mirror back into frame.

Artist: Cindy Gorder

OCEAN WAVE
tray

Combining foil with wire and beads produces a tray that adds a perfect accent to any table or shelf. Serve from this tray and your guests will be amazed and delighted with your talent.

MATERIALS	
• Acrylic tray • Medium and light blue foil • 18-gauge and 22-gauge wire in several shades of blue • Blue and green E beads • Seashells	• Double-sided tape • Glass adhesive • Round-nose pliers • Embossing tool • Scissors

1. Using the scissors, cut the medium blue foil to fit the bottom of the tray. Cut a curve from the light blue foil, and fold the cut edge back. Use the double-sided tape to adhere the wrong side of the curve to the right side of the medium blue foil sheet. Turn back and apply tape to all edges. Adhere the two pieces of foil to the tray, and emboss wavy spirals onto them using the embossing tool.

2. Make single and double spirals from all of colors of 18-gauge wire. Connect the spirals into a mat using the 22-gauge wire. The mat should be slightly smaller than the bottom of the tray. String the E beads onto the wires around the outside edges of the mat.

3. Glue some seashells and wire spirals to the top edge of the tray with glass adhesive for a whimsical touch.

GOLDEN
candle collar

Reflect flickering candlelight for a romantic touch with this gold foil candle collar. You can make candle collars to fit any size and shape of candlestick, giving them style even when the candles aren't lit.

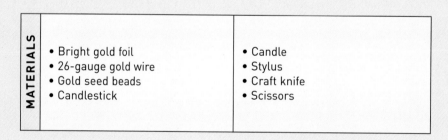

MATERIALS		
• Bright gold foil • 26-gauge gold wire • Gold seed beads • Candlestick	• Candle • Stylus • Craft knife • Scissors	

1. Using the scissors, cut two collars with radiating points from the gold foil. Use the craft knife to cut out a hole large enough to insert the candle in the center of each collar. Emboss the collars with the stylus.

2. Add some beads to various lengths of wire, to your liking. Make holes for the beaded wires in the collars, as desired, with an awl or the point of a craft knife. Add the beaded wire to the collars.

3. Wrap the beaded wire around the candle base. Insert a candle into the candlestick through collars.

Artist: Debba Haupert

RUSTIC WOOD-BURNED AND FOILED
tray

This project provides an excellent example of combining mediums and techniques. It also illustrates the versatility of working with metal foils. The warmth of the wood-burned designs is beautifully reflected in the stamped-foil motifs.

MATERIALS		
	• Wooden tray • Wood burner • Medium-weight gold tooling foil • Rubber stamps and ink pad • Gel stain	• Embossing tool • Water-based varnish, satin finish • Wood glue • Scissors • White plastic eraser

1. Stamp the tray in a design to your taste. Then, using the stamped designs as a pattern, burn the designs into the tray with the wood burner.

2. Stain and varnish the tray.

3. Stamp the foil, and, again using the stamped design as a pattern, emboss the foil from the backside to create raised embossing. Fill the depressions with wood glue, and allow the glue to dry.

4. Using the scissors, cut out the foil pieces, and glue them to the tray.

Artist: Betty Auth

STILETTO
photo holder

Have a blast kicking up your heels with this project. Can you imagine a better use for that "killer" pair of heels sitting in the closet? This project is perfect on a dressing table or bureau to hold snapshots of friends and family.

MATERIALS		
• 3 sheets red foil • Xyron 850 machine fitted with adhesive-only cartridge • Unused high-heeled shoe • Air-dry clay • Scissors	• 18-gauge silver wire • 22-gauge silver wire • Pliers • Glass adhesive • Assorted red and silver beads	

1. Apply the adhesive to the wrong side of two sheets of foil using the Xyron machine, following manufacturer's directions.

2. Cover the shoe with the foil. Press some air-dry clay into the inside of the shoe.

3. Bend the 18-gauge silver wire into five spirals of different lengths. Place the remaining sheet of red foil over the shoe opening. Insert the points of the spirals into the clay, and allow the clay to completely dry.

4. String some beads onto the 22-gauge wire. Twist the wire around the shoe, allowing occasional fingers of wire to bend over inside shoe. Glue the wire fingers inside shoe with adhesive, and allow it to dry.

5. Trim any excess foil close to the shoe with the scissors, allowing a few ½" (1.3 cm) tabs to tuck inside the shoe. Glue the tabs inside shoe with adhesive, and let dry.

Artist: Beth Wheeler

IMAGE TRANSFER
album

Display a favorite photograph using this unusual technique that transfers an image onto foil. This album features a quiet and sophisticated design, allowing it to fit into any decorating style.

MATERIALS		
	• 4 sheets of silver-colored foil • Sheet of decal medium • Xyron machine with adhesive-only cartridge • Photo album	• Chipboard or noncorrugated cardboard • Scissors • Favorite photo

1. Apply adhesive to the back of three sheets silver foil using the Xyron machine. Cover the front, spine, and back of the photo album with the silver foil

2. Photocopy a favorite photo onto the decal medium, following the manufacturer's directions. Transfer the photo decal to the remaining sheet of silver foil. Allow it to dry and cure completely.

3. Apply adhesive to the back of the sheet of silver foil with photo decal.

4. Using the scissors, trim the chipboard to the same size as the photo album. Cover the chipboard with the photo decal.

5. Apply adhesive to the back of the covered chipboard, and mount it on the front of the photo album.

Artist: Beth Wheeler

patterns

This chapter contains patterns you can use to guide you through the projects.
For the best results, photocopy the patterns, and then shrink or enlarge them
as necessary.

Pattern for Herb Tags on page 28

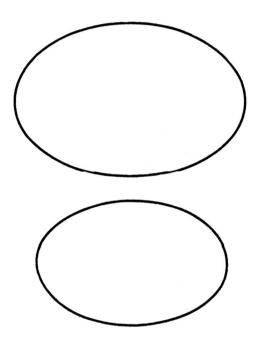

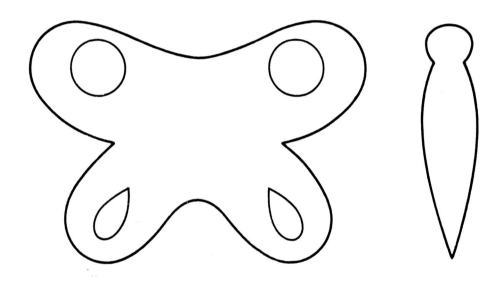

resources

METAL FOIL GIFTS
page 20
Festive Bottle Wraps
Reynolds Bright Ideas Ultra Foil
Toner Fun Wire
Fiskars tools

page 24
Dangling Wine Glass Charms
Amaco ArtEmboss foil
Toner Fun Wire
Fiskars tools

page 28
Herb Tags
St. Louis Metals tooling foil
Toner Fun Wire
Fiskars tools

page 32
Butterfly Plant Pokes
Reynolds Bright Ideas Ultra Foil
Toner Fun Wire
Xyron machine
Fiskars tools

page 36
Foil-Embellished Journal
Magic Metal from ArtSeeds.com
Fiskars tools
Stampendous rubber stamps
Ranger Décor It ink
Glass, Beads & More from
    Beacon Adhesives

WALL DECORATIONS
page 42
Faux Tin Tile Framed Mirror
Reynolds Bright Ideas Ultra Foil
Reynolds Bright Ideas double-sided tape
    and embossing tool
Plaid Paint for Plastic
Rub'n Buff paint

page 46
Sparkling Window Valance
Classic aluminum foil
Artistic wire
McGill giant circle punch
Micro punch
EmbossArt design unit die

page 50
Rustic Charm Wall Pocket
Down Memory Lane Quick Rust steel
Toner Fun Wire
Krylon Crystal Clear Matte Coating
Fiskars tools

page 54
Metallic Galaxy Ornaments
AmacoArtEmboss foil
St. Louis Crafts Inc. aluminum tool foil
Toner Fun Wire
Fiskars tools

page 58
Red Heart Sconce
Amaco ArtEmboss foil
WireForm armature wire
Artistic Wire

page 62
Funky-Footed Frame
Amaco ArtEmboss foil
Fimo clay
E-6000 glue

ALL AROUND THE HOUSE
page 68
Foil-Covered Flower Holder
Maid O' Metal foil
Toner Fun Wire
Fiskars tools

page 72
Moroccan Mosaic Vase
Reynolds Bright Ideas Ultra Foil
Plaid Paint for Plastic
Paper Adventures Lil' Boss diamond
embosser
Mosaics & More from Beacon Adhesives

page 76
Stars and Moon Mobile
Reynolds Bright Ideas Ultra Foil
Marvy Uchida punches
Xyron machine
Fiskars tools

page 80
Metallic Lamp Shade
Reynolds Bright Ideas Ultra Foil and
    double-sided tape
Fiskars tools
Xyron machine

manufacturers & distributors

ASSORTED SUPPLIES
Allcrafts
P.O. Box 7
Bullcreek, WA 6149
Australia
Phone: (08)9310 7884
www.allcrafts.com

HobbyCraft
Bournemouth, UK
Phone: +01202 596100

John Lewis
Oxford Street
London, W1A 1EX, UK
Phone: +02172 697711
www.johnlewis.co.uk

FOIL
Amaco
American Art Clay Co., Inc.
4717 W. Sixteenth St.
Indianapolis, IN 46222
Phone: (317) 244-6871, (800) 374-1600
www.amaco.com

Amaco (European Office)
P.O. Box 467
Longton, Stoke-On-Trent
ST3 7DN, UK
Phone: +01782 399219

Craft Catalog
P.O. Box 1069
Reynoldsburg, OH 43068
Phone: (800) 777-1442
www.craftcatalog.com

Reynolds Consumer Products
Richmond, VA 23261
www.reynoldscrafts.com

WIRE
Artistic Wire
1210 Harrison Ave.
La Grange Park, IL 60526
Phone: (630) 530-7567
www.artisticwire.com

Toner Fun Wire
699 Silver St.
Agawam, MA 01001
Phone: (413) 789-1300
www.tonerplastics.com

TOOLS
EK Success
P.O. Box 1141
Clifton, NJ 07014
Phone: (973) 458-0092
www.eksuccess.com

Fiskars, Inc.
7811 W. Stewart Ave.
Wausau, WI 54401
Phone: (800) 950-0203
www.fiskars.com

McGill, Inc.
131 E. Prairie St.
P.O. Box 177
Marengo, IL 60152
www.mcgillinc.com

Xyron, Inc.
15820 N. 84th St.
Scottsdale, AZ 85260
Phone: (800) 793-3523
www.xyron.com

PAINTS AND PIGMENTS
Jacquard Products
Phone: (707) 433-9577
www.jacquardproducts.com

Rupert, Gibbon & Spider, Inc.
P.O. Box 425
Healdsburg, CA 95448
Phone: (800) 442-0455

Plaid Enterprises, Inc
P.O. Box 7600
Norcross, GA 30091-7600
Phone: (678) 291-8174
www.plaidonline.com

SURFACES
Design A Line Inc.
Kreative Foam
1376 S. Battalion Bay
Saratoga Springs, UT 84043
Phone: (801) 766-8551
www.Design-a-line.com

The Craf-T-Pedlars
A division of The Basket Pedlars
1009-D Shary Circle
Concord, CA 94518
Phone: (877) 733-5277
www.pedlars.com

MADELINE ARENDT

Madeline Arendt has been an avid designer and crafter for over 30 years. An accomplished teacher, she shares her love of every crafting media with students from all walks of life. Her friends call her "Martha," whereas she calls herself "a jack-of-all-trades, a master of some."

BETTY AUTH

Betty Auth is a woodburning artist, designer, and author who loves experimenting with rubber stamps and using her creativity in many different media. Her most recent book is *Stamping Tricks for Scrapbooks*, Rockport Publishers, 2002. She is also the author of *The Art of Woodburning*, Sterling Publishing, 2001, and *Woodburning*, a Weekend Crafter book from Lark Books, 1999. Betty is the author of many magazine projects, articles, and features, as well as numerous online and television features. She can be reached at Auth-Antic Designs, bauth@houston.rr.com, or by phone at (281) 879-0430.

CINDY GORDER

Cindy Gorder is a graphic artist and published craft-project designer, specializing in "crazy-quilting," beadwork, paper crafts, wire, decoupage, collage, stamping, and polymer clay—but she can't resist dabbling in other media from time to time. She lives in rural Wisconsin on a dairy farm, which her husband operates.

DEBBA HAUPERT

Debba Haupert shares her home in Cincinnati, Ohio, with her wonderful husband, very spoiled dog, and lazy cat. She supports her craft habit through craft designing and freelance marketing for the craft industry. Her artist mother, loyal friends, and kind fellow designers thankfully fill her days with laughter, inspiration, and support.

ALBA MONROS

Alba Monros was born into a family of renowned artists and sculptors. Surrounded by an abundance of art supplies, patience, and inspiration, Alba has been an artist all of her life. Paper, polymer clay, rubber stamps, wire, and metal foil are her favorites, but she has been known to work in virtually every medium. Alba generously shares her love of everything artistic with her enthusiastic students.

contributing artists—continued

KATHY PETERSON

Kathy Peterson has authored three books. Her work has been published in numerous magazines and books, and has been featured on *The Christopher Lowell Show, The Carol Duvall Show, Home Matters, Today at Home, Decorating With Style*, and many more. Kathy lives in Tequesta, Florida, where she produces and hosts her own national TV show, *Town & Country Crafts with Kathy Peterson*. For more information about Kathy, please visit her Web site at www.kathypeterson.com.

KELLEY R. TAYLOR

Kelley R. Taylor is a freelance craft and home decor designer. Her work can be found in several books, magazines, and Web sites, and is featured each week on CreatingHomeDecor.com, the resource for the do-it-yourself decorator.

BETH WHEELER

Beth Wheeler has published hundreds of articles, how-to project designs, and books for quilting, sewing, craft, and folk-art audiences, and often writes business-oriented articles for craft trade publications. She is a member of the Board of Directors for the Society of Craft Designers (SCD), the Association of Crafts and Creative Industries (ACCI), and the Hobby Industry Association (HIA), and a past member of the Board of Directors for the Virginia Quilt Museum. Located near Washington, D.C., Beth's company, Beth Wheeler Creative Services, provides consulting, promotional, and product-development services to manufacturers, publishers, and corporate clients in the creative industries. A strong proponent of crafting with children, Beth believes there are rewards for both children and the adults who teach them. She speaks often to children's groups about "life in the craft lane." Beth lives with her husband, Geoff, and Scottish terrier, Kippy, in a three-story townhouse, which is happily crowded with fabrics, books, supplies, and projects in progress.

BARBARA MATTHIESSEN is a familiar name in the design world. She has authored 37 craft booklets and over 2,000 magazine articles. She has also contributed her artwork to 12 hardcover craft books. A member of the Society of Craft Designers, she has done product development and consulting for numerous manufacturers, craft retailers, and Web sites. She lives in Port Orchard, Washington.

acknowledgments

I would like to thank a number of people whose contributions have made this book possible. First, I'd like to thank Mary Ann Hall, my editor, for her wise guidance, infinite patience, and artistic vision. As a talented designer and author in her own right, Mary Ann's insights were extremely valuable to all aspects of this book. I am grateful to Winnie Prentiss, Claire MacMaster, Pamela Hunt, and the entire Rockport team who used their talents to pull this book together. Thank you all very much.

I also want to thank all of the artists who contributed projects and gallery pieces. All of you did magnificent work and were a joy to work with. Many thanks to Kathy Peterson, Deborah Haupert, and Alba Monros for their wonderful step-by-step projects. And thanks very much to Betty Auth, Madeline Arendt, Cindy Gorder, Kelly R. Taylor, and Beth Wheeler for their fantastic contributions to the gallery section of this book.

Sincere appreciation to Lynda Musante at Reynolds Bright Ideas and Mark Hill at Amaco for providing an abundance of metal foils to the designers and for lending their support to this project. I'd also like to thank Tracia Williams from Toner Plastics and Julianna Hudgins from Artistic Wire for providing the generous amounts of wire used in this book. Thanks to Sandra Cashman and Barb Lashua at Fiskars for supplying amazing tools.

Lastly, I'd like to thank my friends and family who put up with my creative "storms" when I have projects and pieces of projects everywhere and can't be bothered to answer the phone, let alone cook a meal. Most of all I want to thank my husband, Larry, who is infinitely patient, understanding, and supportive.